D1295371

Giant Leaps

The Mercury Seven

Stuart A. Kallen

ABDO & Daughters
PUBLISHING

SAYVILLE LIBRARY

Published by Abdo & Daughters, 4940 Viking Dr., Suite 622, Edina, MN 55435.

Copyright ©1996 by Abdo Consulting Group, Inc., Pentagon Tower, P.O. Box 36036, Minneapolis, Minnesota 55435. International copyrights reserved in all countries. No part of this book may be reproduced in any form without written permission from the publisher. Printed in the United States.

Cover Photos by: Archive Photos
Inside Photos by:
Archive Photos: 4-5, 7, 8, 19
AP/Wide World Photos: 7, 15
Bettmann: 11, 12, 13, 14, 16, 17, 21, 23, 25, 26, 27, 28

Edited by Bob Italia

Library of Congress Cataloging–in–Publication Data
Kallen, Stuart A.,
The Mercury seven / Stuart A. Kallen
    p. cm. — (Giant leaps)
Includes bibliographical references and index.
Summary: Describes the early efforts of the Soviet Union and the United States to be the first to put a man into space, focusing on the early missions of Project Mercury.
   ISBN 1-56239-565-3
   1. Project Mercury (U.S.)—Juvenile literature. 2. Space race—United States—History—Juvenile literature. 3. Space race—Soviet Union—History—Juvenile literature. [l. Space race. 2. Project Mercury (U.S.)] I. Title. II. Series.
   TL789.8.U6M474 1996
   629.45' 0973—dc20   95-33385
                                                                                    CIP
                                                                                    AC

CONTENTS

THE STORY OF PROJECT MERCURY

SINCE THE BEGINNING OF time, human beings have dreamt of walking through space. To the ancient Romans, that dream was given form in their god of science, Mercury. Mercury had wings on his feet to fly through the heavens. Over the centuries, great empires rose and fell, but no human could ever put on wings and fly far into space like Mercury. That is, until April 12, 1961, when the Soviet Union put Cosmonaut Yuri Gagarin into outer space aboard the *Vostok 1*.

Gagarin was inside a space capsule attached to a 126-foot (38.4 meter) long, 320-ton (290 metric ton) rocket. By igniting large amounts of liquid oxygen and kerosene, the Soviets broke the bounds of the earth and shot a man into space.

At the time, there was great mistrust between the Soviet Union and the United States. After World War II ended in 1945, the Soviets

This page: Astronaut John Glenn, the first American to orbit the earth, experiences weightlessness in space.

took over most of Eastern Europe. Americans felt the Soviets wanted to take over the entire world. Both countries began building bigger and bigger nuclear bombs and huge rockets to launch them. The battle was a stand-off. Both sides had hundreds of nuclear missiles pointed at each other. Many smaller countries joined the battle, picking one side or the other to support. This era was called the Cold War. It began in 1945 and lasted until the Communist government of the Soviet Union collapsed in 1991.

The armies of both countries prepared for the final nuclear war they hoped would never be fought. While this happened, new uses were found for the missiles and rockets that were built to carry nuclear weapons. They could also carry human beings into space—even to the moon. This centuries-old dream became a race to space between the U.S. and the Soviet Union.

The Soviets won the first leg of the race when they put the first satellite in orbit on October 4, 1957. The tiny, 184-pound (83 kilogram), unmanned spacecraft was called *Sputnik*. It circled the earth once every 96 minutes. *Sputnik* put the Americans on notice that they had better launch their own satellites, or soon the Soviets would control outer space. They might use that control to spy on the United States or even drop bombs. On November 3, the Soviets sent a small dog, named Laika, into space to test conditions for manned spacecraft.

Fortunately the United States had the talent to meet the Soviet challenge. Wernher von Braun had been working to build rockets for the Army. Von Braun was a German rocket scientist who had helped Germany build "Vengeance Weapon 2" (V-2) rockets during World War II. When Germany lost the war, von Braun defected to the U.S. The V-2s were the first bombs to use liquid fuel (gasoline and liquid oxygen) propellant. Before the V-2, rockets used solid fuel such as gunpowder.

When von Braun came to the United States after the war, he made bigger and bigger missiles. By the time the Soviets launched *Sputnik,* von Braun had developed the massive Jupiter-C rocket. On January 31, 1958, the United States launched a satellite called *Explorer I* from Cape Canaveral in Florida. Soon the U.S. and the Soviet Union were racing to put more and more satellites in space.

On July 29, 1958, United States President Dwight D. Eisenhower signed the National Aeronautics and Space Act (NASA). This created the space agency NASA, which took over some test centers in Virginia, California, and at Cape Canaveral, Florida. NASA also constructed a new research center in Maryland called the Goddard Space Flight Center. T. Keith Glennan ran the new space agency.

By 1959, the Americans and the Soviets built bigger and better satellites. They were even sending crude robot probes to other planets. The next step was manned flight. NASA called its manned space program Mercury, after the Roman messenger of the gods.

NASA's first job was to design a capsule that would protect humans from all phases of spaceflight. The dangers included the incredible launch speeds, weightlessness in space, the furnace-like heat of

Right: A German V-2 rocket lifts off. *Right below:* The Roman god Mercury.

reentry, and a 10,000-foot (3,100 meters) parachute landing. The capsule had to weigh less than 3,000 pounds (1,359 kilograms).

NASA's designers built a capsule that looked like an upside-down badminton "birdie." The blunt bottom was a fiberglass heat shield. This would point the way during reentry when temperatures rose to thousands of degrees. A cluster of small retrorockets would break the capsule from orbital speeds and return it to earth. The tiny cabin was topped with a cone that held radio antennas and parachutes. The capsule's pilot would lie flat on his back on a padded, formed couch. In early 1959, McDonnell Aircraft Corporation won the contract to build Mercury spacecraft. Soon they produced a full-scale mock-up.

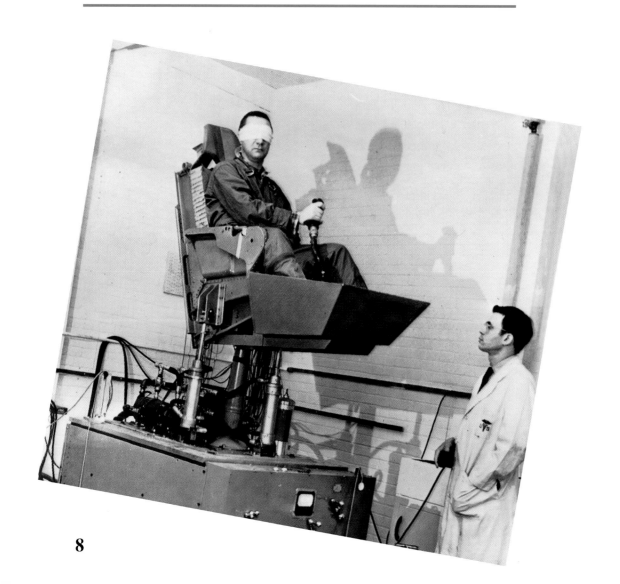

THE STAR TRAVELERS

While the capsule was under production, NASA had to select people to fly the Mercury spacecraft. Some wanted "seekers of danger"— daredevils such as mountain climbers, skydivers, even bullfighters. President Eisenhower wanted military test pilots. They had courage, technical knowledge, and they were cleared for top secret projects. The Pentagon pulled a list of 110 qualified men (all Defense Department pilots were men at that time). NASA would pick six.

All pilots needed a university degree in the physical sciences or engineering, and 1,500 hours of flight time. They had to be less than 40 years old, and less than 5 feet, 11 inches (1.8 meters) tall. The new breed of pilot would be called an *astronaut*—Latin for *star traveler*.

Left: Air Force Captain Virgil "Gus" Grissom is blindfolded as he "flies" a simulator in a test used to pick the Project Mercury astronauts.

The Pentagon settled on 32 semifinalists. These men were then put through extreme tests to find out their physical and mental condition. Some called it "scientific torture."

The men were shaken, spun, jolted, frozen, and baked. They ran on treadmills until they dropped. At the same time, NASA psychologists questioned them for hours, searching for mental flaws. Finally a board of senior engineers, flight surgeons, psychologists, and psychiatrists made the selection. But the board could not agree on which six to choose. So the astronaut pool was expanded to seven.

On April 9, 1959, reporters and television cameras crowded into a room in Washington, D.C. At 2 p.m., NASA's Glennan walked in to face the media. Behind him were seven young men with flattop haircuts. The men walked with a calm confidence. Cameras and TV lights glared.

Glennan said, "Today we are introducing to you and the world these seven young men who have been selected to begin training for orbital spaceflight...the nation's Mercury astronauts!"

The reporters rose to their feet, cheered, and clapped. The seven men grinned. On the table before them sat a model of the Mercury capsule atop its Atlas rocket booster.

The men stood one by one and introduced themselves. Each one got a round of applause. There was senior officer John Glenn, the oldest at 37. He was an experienced Marine pilot with 5,000 flight hours. Glenn saw combat in World War II and the Korean War.

Malcom Scott Carpenter was a 33-year-old Navy pilot. Walter Schirra was 36, and a lieutenant commander in the Navy. Alan Shepard was another Navy pilot, also 36, who had graduated near the top of his class at Annapolis. Virgil (Gus) Grissom was a captain in the Air Force. He was 33 and had flown over 100 combat missions over Korea. Captain Donald (Deke) Slayton was 35 and had flown bombers in World War II. He worked for Boeing as an aeronautical engineer. The youngest astronaut was 32-year-old Leroy Gordon Cooper, an Air Force captain. He test piloted in the most advanced

fighters at Edwards Air Force Base in California. All seven astronauts were married with children.

Several of America's leading test pilots could not even apply for the job. Chuck Yeager, who had the world speed record, did not have a science or engineering degree. Still, the Mercury Seven were among the world's top pilots.

Right: The Mercury Seven astronauts. From left to right: Navy Lt. Comdr. Walter M. Schirra, Jr.; Navy Lt. Comdr. Alan B. Shepard, Jr.; Air Force Capt. Virgil I. (Gus) Grissom; Air Force Capt. Donald (Deke) K. Slayton; Marine Lt. Col. John H. Glenn, Jr.; Navy Lt. Malcolm Scott Carpenter; and Air Force Capt. Leroy G. (Gordo) Cooper, Jr.

SAYVILLE LIBRARY

11

THE COUNTDOWN BEGINS

On July 1, 1960, Wernher von Braun was transferred from the Army Ballistic Missile Agency to NASA. He became director of NASA's new Marshall Space Flight Center in Huntsville, Alabama. There, von Braun had a rocket laboratory like nothing ever seen before. His team could build rocket boosters, satellites, and spacecraft.

The first Mercury flight would be unmanned. During the summer of 1960, the launch was scheduled, canceled, and scheduled again. The press and the public grew impatient.

At 9:13 a.m. on July 29, a shiny white Atlas missile roared to life with the dull black Mercury capsule atop it. Within seconds it disappeared into the sky over Cape Canaveral. After 58 seconds, the tracking screens in Mission Control went dead. A naval unit reported debris raining down into the ocean. The Atlas rocket had exploded at 32,000 feet (9,920 meters). It had been traveling at 1,400 feet (434 meters) per *second*. The flight tech's nightmares had come true. The Atlas rocket could not safely launch the Mercury capsule. If an astronaut had been aboard, he would have died. *Time* magazine mocked the flight, calling it "Lead-Footed Mercury."

A New President, a New Breakthrough

The Mercury explosion took place in an election year. Democratic presidential nominee John F. Kennedy hammered away at Eisenhower for letting the Soviets challenge America's leadership in space. Kennedy vowed that, if elected, he would never let the Soviet Union embarrass the U.S. again.

A few months later, another Atlas missile exploded in a widely televised failure. Meanwhile the Soviets had launched a satellite with two dogs aboard. It was four times heavier than Mercury. Soviet

President Kennedy

This page: Flames erupt from a Vanguard missile as it starts to fall over on its side after exploding two seconds after liftoff. The missile rose four feet (1.2 meters) before the blast rocked its first two stages.

leader Nikita Khrushchev held a press conference. He announced that the Soviet Union would soon put a man in space.

John F. Kennedy was elected president of the U.S. in November 1960. On election day, another Mercury capsule failed 16 seconds after its launch.

After another failure in November, von Braun's team finally

Ham.

put an unmanned Mercury capsule into space. On January 31, 1961, NASA launched a Mercury capsule with a 37-pound (16-kilogram) chimpanzee named "Ham" riding on his own custom couch. The "monkeynaut" returned to earth in good spirits. He ate an apple and an orange while posing for pictures. Von Braun planned to launch an astronaut in April.

THE LAUNCH OF VOSTOK

The Soviet Union had been launching several heavy spacecrafts called *Vostok* ("the East") with dogs on board. The Soviet space modules were different from the American's. Because of their desire for secrecy, they did not want their spacecraft landing in international waters, but on the soil of "Mother Russia." That meant the module had to come down on dry land. Men on the ground would control the craft. The cosmonaut would simply help steer. The Vostok capsules were in two parts. One part held the instruments, like batteries, retrorockets, and life-support systems. The other part held a round, reentry module with the cosmonaut. The instrument capsule would burn up upon reentry.

The Vostok reentry sphere would plunge like a fiery cannonball into the earth's atmosphere. When it was five miles (eight kilometers) above earth, the hatch would automatically blow. The cosmonaut would then parachute to earth in an ejection seat, like those used in fighter jets.

While experimenting with an unmanned Vostok flight, the head Soviet rocket scientist, Sergei Korolev, suffered a heart attack. But he would not let that stop him. He left the hospital after one week and resumed his 18-hour-a-day work schedule. To beat the Mercury astronauts into space, the Soviets speeded up their program.

The first Vostok cosmonaut, Pyotr Dolgov, died during reentry. His space suit did not fit through the hatch opening. The next hatch design was bigger.

On April 12, 1961, the Soviet Union announced to the world: "The world's first spaceship, *Vostok*, the *East*, with a man on board, has been launched in the Soviet Union on a round-the-world orbit." The cosmonaut was 27-year-old Air Force Major Yuri Gagarin. The flight had been launched at 9:07 a.m. Moscow time. For less than two hours, bulletins on Radio Moscow traced *Vostok*'s flight across the sky. At 10:55 a.m., Gagarin returned safely to earth.

Below: Soviet Cosmonaut Yuri A. Gagarin and the *Vostok I* rocket, which carried him on his historic trip to become the first man to rocket into space.

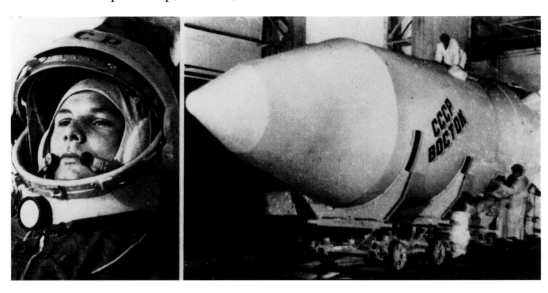

FLIGHT OF *FREEDOM 7*

The Soviet Union had launched the world's first satellite. Now they had put a man into space. Once again, they had beaten the Americans. A huge cry rose up from the press, politicians, and the public. American honor was at stake.

On May 5, 1961, almost 1,000 reporters and TV crews gathered at Cape Canaveral. NASA was finally ready to launch a Mercury astronaut into space. Navy Lieutenant Commander Alan B. Shepard, Jr., had been chosen to ride the first manned Mercury mission.

Shepard dressed in his gleaming foil-skin space suit. He rode the open cage elevator to the top of the tower where he climbed into the Mercury capsule. Around 6:00 a.m., Shepard was strapped onto the couch and the door was bolted. Shepard had named the Mercury spacecraft *Freedom 7*.

After three hours of last-minute delays, Mercury was ready to fly. Forty-five million Americans watched on their televisions. The slender 70-foot (21.7-meter), black-and-white booster rocket gleamed in the sun. Twenty-five tons (22.6 metric tons) of explosive propellant sat quietly under the astronaut.

Shepard was so excited that he did not hear the final moments of the countdown. Liftoff was smooth for the first minute. But soon the capsule rocked with vibrations caused by the incredible speed. Shepard's head slammed against the couch even though he was strapped down. Two minutes into the trip, the Mercury capsule sped to 5,134 miles (8,260 kilometers) per hour. Shepard was in the zero gravity of space.

When *Freedom 7* reached 117 miles (188 kilometers) above Florida,

Above: Commander Alan Shepard leaving the hanger on his way to the Mercury capsule. *Right:* The Redstone rocket blasts off with the Mercury capsule carrying Shepard on America's first spaceflight.

16

Shepard took over the controls to fly the spacecraft. He turned the Mercury capsule and blasted the retrorockets. At 10,000 feet (16,090 meters) above earth, the small parachute opened. The capsule soon splashed down into the Atlantic Ocean, 302 miles (496 kilometers) east of Cape Canaveral.

A Marine helicopter pulled Shepard from the ocean. Soon he was talking to the president. America had put a man in space. The whole world had seen it. President Kennedy was very happy.

BOLD PLAN FOR THE FUTURE

On May 25, 1961, Kennedy addressed a joint session of Congress. Kennedy spoke about the struggle between American liberty and Soviet dictatorship. Then Kennedy said: "It is time for a new American enterprise...I believe that this nation should commit itself to achieving the goal, before this decade is out, of landing a man on the moon and returning him safely to earth. No single space project in this period will be more exciting, or more impressive to mankind, or more important for the long-range exploration of space; and none will be so difficult and expensive to accomplish."

Kennedy put the price tag at $40 billion. It would be expensive. But Kennedy added: "If we are to go only halfway, or reduce our sights in the face of difficulty, it would be better not to go at all."

America was swept up in the idea of space travel. Fighter pilots went to college with the hopes of becoming astronauts. Plans were drawn up to send a man to Mars. Colleges and university research departments began designing interplanetary spacecraft. New words crept into the English language that were straight out of NASA—glitch, systems go, liftoff, splashdown, and A-OK.

Right: Project Mercury's Control Center at Cape Canaveral, Florida. The display shows the capsule's position.

18

NASA planned another manned Mercury flight. The press followed the program as if it were a major sporting event. Reporters swarmed around astronauts. TV crews followed them around Cape Canaveral. Gus Grissom was the next man to fly Mercury. He called the capsule *Liberty Bell 7*.

The capsule had been redesigned by request from the astronauts. The tiny port-hole windows were enlarged. The hatch was modified to allow a quick escape during splashdown. Other changes were made to make the ride smoother.

After several days of rain, delaying the launch, Gus Grissom finally climbed into *Liberty Bell 7* on July 21. At 7:20 a.m., the capsule lifted off. The padding on Grissom's couch was thicker, so he wasn't pounded around like Shepard had been. Two minutes and 22 seconds later, Grissom was in space. Minutes later a light blinked on the control panel. *Liberty Bell* was at an altitude of 118 miles (190 kilometers).

Grissom fired the retros. But the capsule tumbled out of control. His heart was racing and he could not talk. Colored smoke from the

blazing reentry shield billowed past the window. Finally the parachute opened, 12,000 feet (3,720 meters) above earth. But there was a tear in the orange and white chute. Grissom prayed it would not grow bigger.

Four minutes later, the landing bag inflated and the capsule splashed down hard into the ocean. *Liberty Bell* tipped over. Grissom stared out at the inky depths of the Atlantic Ocean through the window. He heard a dull thud. The hatch had blown off. A warm wave flooded the cockpit. *Liberty Bell* rolled over again. Another wave surged in. The capsule began to sink. Grissom struggled out of the capsule. He was directly under the blasting rotor of the rescue helicopter. The chopper tried to rescue the sinking capsule. But it pulled the chopper down with it. The helicopter almost went into the water.

Grissom was in serious danger. His suit was flooding. As he thrashed his arms, the suit sucked in more seawater. He screamed for help. His cries disappeared into the noise of the helicopter. At the last moment, a backup chopper tossed Grissom a rescue sling. He put it on, but went under water. Soon he was jerked into the bright sunlight. He twirled under the chopper like a fish on a line.

Grissom was saved seconds before drowning. *Liberty Bell* sank almost 18,000 feet (5,580 meters) below the surface.

Grissom was safe. But the technical difficulties had almost killed him. In spite of the incident, NASA felt that the Mercury system was "spaceworthy." American astronauts could survive the stress of flight. The next hurdle was orbital flight—to send a capsule around the earth, using the Atlas booster rocket.

Gus Grissom's luck did not improve. He died on January 27, 1967, when a fire broke out in the command module of the first Apollo mission while the capsule was still on the ground.

Right: The Soviet Union's second cosmonaut, Gherman Titov, getting into the capsule that will carry him in orbit 17 times around the earth.

AROUND THE WORLD

Soviet Union leader Khrushchev was not happy about Mercury's success. He ordered Korolev to speed up the Vostok program and put another man into orbit. Korolev said the Vostok was unsafe to challenge Mercury. Khrushchev did not care. He ordered a Vostok mission to orbit earth 17 times. Korolev said that his retrorockets might fail after such a long time in space. That would leave a cosmonaut in orbit with no way to return to earth. Khrushchev ordered a flight of *Vostok 2* for August.

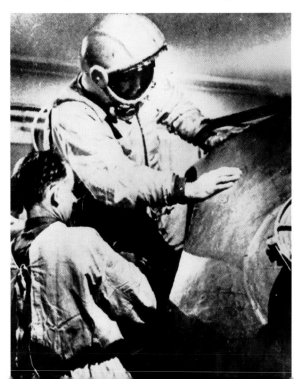

On August 6, 1961, Soviet Air Force Major Gherman Titov put on his bright orange space suit. He climbed through the hatch of the *Vostok 2*. A rocket launched him into the clear blue sky of the Soviet republic of Kazakhastan.

During the first five hours of the flight, nothing happened. Titov had lunch which he squeezed from plastic tubes. By afternoon, Titov felt seasick. His instrument panel seemed to bob up and down and swim before his eyes. He felt he was flying upside down. Soon, Titov turned down the cabin lights and told controllers he was going to sleep. Hours later, Titov finally made it back to earth safely.

The next day, the still-sick Titov was shown to the world, standing next to Khrushchev. Titov had orbited the earth 17 times in 25 hours, 18 minutes. He had traveled 436,656 miles (703,150 kilometers). Titov had been the first man to orbit the earth 17 times.

21

"THERE'S A REAL FIREBALL OUTSIDE"

In November 1961, NASA launched Mercury-Atlas 5. It was the first orbital flight of an unmanned Mercury capsule. But a monkey rode on board. The same day, NASA announced that Marine Lieutenant Colonel John Glenn would fly Mercury's first manned orbital flight.

In early 1962, thousands of reporters arrived at Cape Canaveral. But January weather caused several flight delays. Other problems pushed the mission back into February. Finally, on February 20, the skies over Florida cleared for a few hours. Glenn climbed into the capsule he named *Friendship 7*.

By 9:47 a.m., Glenn was on his way. He reported severe quaking as the capsule reached orbital speeds. When he was 20 miles (32 kilometers) high the boosters shut down and fell away. The capsule tilted over and Glenn reported: "A beautiful sight, looking eastward across the Atlantic." Soon Glenn did a series of exercises that prevented him from getting spacesickness.

Glenn fired the orbit thrusters and tilted *Friendship* forward. Now he could see the Canary Islands and the sandy Sahara Desert roll by beneath him. Thirty minutes into the launch, he had traveled from Florida to Africa. Glenn circled the earth, marveling at its beauty. The spacecraft behaved perfectly.

After 4 hours, 33 minutes, Glenn positioned the spacecraft so the heat shield faced the California coast. The retrorockets fired. As the spacecraft plunged towards earth, Glenn saw orange and black smoke shoot past his window. Molten drops of metal flew by. The heat shield became white-hot. A moment later, one of the steel straps holding the shield onto the craft burned through. Glenn heard pieces of it brushing against the capsule. He called Mission Control. "There's a real fireball outside," he said. Another red-hot strap broke and flew by the window.

Right: John Glenn in the Mercury capsule *Friendship 7*.

No one could hear Glenn's fearful comments. He was in a radio blackout zone caused by the superhot cone of particles that surround a spacecraft during reentry. *Friendship 7* began to spin wildly. Glenn tried to use thrusters to hold it steady. Just as the capsule was about to tumble out of control, the parachute opened. Glenn was back in the earth's atmosphere. Less than 30 minutes later, he was on the Navy destroyer *Noa*. He grinned as he talked to President Kennedy by radio-telephone. Glenn said that it had been a "wonderful trip, almost unbelievable."

Across America, 100 million people watched Glenn on television. They were proud. Four days later, Glenn was given a standing ovation when he addressed a joint session of Congress. He talked about America's goal of a 1970 moon landing. Four million people lined the streets of New York City two days later. They gave American hero John Glenn a record-breaking ticker-tape parade.

Aurora 7

On May 24, 1962, the space press corps returned to the Cape for the launch of Mercury-Atlas 7. Navy Lieutenant Scott Carpenter would fly the mission. Carpenter had named his capsule *Aurora 7*.

Aurora was in orbit less than six minutes after liftoff. Carpenter was overcome by the beauty of the earth below him. In fact, engineers on the ground had to remind him to quit looking out the window and proceed with experiments. Carpenter wasted fuel trying to perform maneuvers that Glenn had done easily. He even switched on a thruster accidentally. This doubled his fuel consumption.

After three hours, Carpenter was dangerously low on fuel. He shut down the thrusters and drifted. *Aurora* tumbled slowly around the earth for an hour. Carpenter relaxed and photographed the rain forests below him and the quarter moon above him. But then Carpenter fired the retrorockets too late. He made several mistakes. He took over the automatic controls as the thruster fuel was bled away. Off course with empty fuel tanks, he sped into the atmosphere.

The blazing heat of reentry surrounded *Aurora*. The capsule spun out of control and Carpenter had no fuel to stabilize it. Finally the parachute opened and plunked Carpenter down in the Atlantic, 250 miles (402 kilometers) off course. *Aurora* had almost been lost on reentry. Carpenter never flew into space for NASA again.

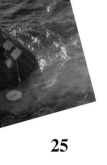

Above: John Glenn stands by as a technician removes an important recording device from *Friendship 7*.

Right: The Mercury capsule in the Atlantic before being picked up by the destroyer *Noa*.

TWO AT A TIME

Khrushchev kept pushing Korolev to outdo the Americans. Korolev couldn't beat Mercury, but he came up with a plan. The Soviets had two Vostok spacecraft already built. Korolev would launch one then launch the other the next day. This would be a "group flight."

On August 11, 1962, *Vostok 3* took off with a cosmonaut on board. Exactly 24 hours, 1 minute, and 4 seconds later, *Vostok 4* blasted off. The second spacecraft fell into orbit 9 miles (15 kilometers) behind the first. This distance was soon reduced to three miles (five kilometers). A TV camera sent scratchy, blurry pictures back, live from *Vostok 4*. It showed a cosmonaut twirling food tubes and small tools in midair. The first TV pictures from space were cut short when the cosmonaut became ill. Three days later, the two Vostoks reentered the atmosphere at the same time. *Vostok 4* landed less than 124 miles (200 kilometers) from *Vostok 3*. The two cosmonauts landed by personal parachute less than six minutes apart. NASA would not attempt such a mission for two years.

Right: A Mercury capsule is fitted onto an Atlas booster at Cape Canaveral, Florida.
Left: Astronaut Wally Schirra is assisted into his *Sigma-7* space capsule early October 3, 1962, in preparation for his six-orbital flight around the earth. During his 9-hour, 13-minute flight, Schirra covered over 160,000 miles (258,000 kilometers), reaching an altitude of 176 miles (283 kilometers).

"BY THE BOOK"

NASA launched Navy Lieutenant Commander Wally Schirra in *Sigma 7* on October 3, 1962. After the flawed Carpenter mission, Schirra said he would fly "by the book," taking no chances. His thruster maneuvers were exact. Like *Vostok 4*, Schirra had a simple TV camera in his capsule. Six hours into the mission, Schirra joked about the full moon being below him and the Rocky Mountains appearing to be above him. Forty million Americans watched on live TV.

Schirra controlled reentry with amazing precision. He landed within five miles (eight kilometers) of the splashdown sight. His flight had been the best so far.

On May 15, 1963, Air Force Major Leroy Gordon "Gordo" Cooper climbed aboard *Faith 7*. It was the final Mercury flight. It was also to be the longest. The launch of *Faith 7* was picture-perfect. After orbiting the earth six times, Gordo went to sleep for eight hours. He had to anchor his thumbs under his chest harness. This kept his hands from floating in zero gravity and accidentally tripping switches on the instrument panel.

At dawn Pacific time the next day, *Faith 7* splashed down less than four miles (6.4 kilometers) from the aircraft carrier *Kearsarge*. Gordo's flight was a success.

The Mercury missions proved that American know-how could put American pilots into orbit and return them safely. NASA was now ready to try more daring manned missions. Among them were deep-space navigation and a lunar landing. The space frontier conquered by the Mercury pilots was now waiting for the Gemini and Apollo missions. By 1969, a human being would walk the surface of the moon.

Below: Astronaut Gordo Cooper emerges from the *Faith 7* space capsule after safely being hauled aboard the aircraft carrier *Kearsarge*.

GLOSSARY

astronaut
A person who is trained for spaceflight. From the Latin words "star traveler."

atmosphere
The gaseous envelope surrounding the earth.

boosters
The first stage of a missile or rocket.

Cape Canaveral
A place on the Atlantic side of Florida where missiles and rockets are launched. Most missions into outer space were launched from Cape Canaveral.

Cold War
A period of strong rivalry between the Soviet Union and the United States that stopped just short of war. This period lasted from 1945 to 1991.

command module
The compartment of a spacecraft that contains the crew and the main controls.

cosmonaut
An astronaut from the Soviet Union.

engineer
A person who makes practical use of pure sciences such as physics and chemistry. Engineers use mathematical and scientific knowledge to build spacecraft.

interplanetary
Between planets.

Kazakhastan
A former republic of the Soviet Union where the Soviets launched their spacecraft.

kerosene
An oily liquid refined from petroleum used as fuel.

liftoff
The start of a rocket's flight from its launch pad, also called "blast off."

liquid fuel rocket
A rocket powered by fuel made of liquid oxygen and kerosene or liquid oxygen and gasoline.

liquid oxygen
Oxygen that is frozen to minus 279 degrees Fahrenheit.

Mission Control
Ground control for spaceflights.

NASA
National Aeronautics and Space Administration. U.S. government agency formed in 1958 to research and launch satellites and spacecraft.

orbit
The path of a satellite or spacecraft.

Pentagon
The United States Department of Defense including the Army, Navy, Air Force, and Marines so called because of the five-sided building that is the headquarters for the departments.

propellant
Fuel that propels, or fires, a rocket.

radio blackout zone
A time during the landing of a spacecraft when communication with the ground is made impossible by heat generated from the landing craft's reentry into the atmosphere.

retro rocket
A small rocket that slows down a spacecraft.

satellite
An object that orbits around a planet.

Soviet Union
A country of 15 republics in Eastern Europe that was ruled by a Communist government. The Soviet Union was disbanded in 1991 and replaced by the Commonwealth of Independent States. Often called Russia.

splashdown
The landing of a space vehicle in the ocean.

Sputnik
A man-made satellite launched by the Soviet Union, means "fellow traveler" in Russian.

systems go
All systems needed to launch a rocket are A-OK.

thruster
A rocket engine that steers a spacecraft.

V-2

"Vengence Weapon 2," the first missile powered by liquid oxygen and kerosene, used by the Nazis in World War II. The V-2 design was later improved for use in launching spacecraft.

Vostok

Name of the first manned spacecraft launched by the Soviet Union. Means "the East" in Russian, the official language of the Soviet Union.

warhead

The forward section of a missile that carries a bomb.

weightlessness

A state of floating experienced in a spacecraft when it is in orbit. Weightlessness is caused by being out in space, far from the pull of the earth's gravity.

zero gravity

Having zero gravitational pull. Weightlessness.

BIBLIOGRAPHY

Aldrin, Buzz. *Men From Earth*. New York: Bantam Books, 1989.

Arco Publishing. *Out of This World*. New York: Arco Publishing, 1985.

Dolan, Edward F. *Famous Firsts in Space*. New York: Cobblehill Books, 1989.

Gatland, Kenneth. *The Illustrated Encyclopedia of Space Technology*. New York: Orion Books, 1989.

Kennedy, Gregory P. *The First Men in Space*. New York: Chelsea House Publishers, 1991.

Olney, Ross Robert. *American in Space*. New York: Thomas Nelson, Inc., 1970.

Pogue, William R. *How Do You Go To The Bathroom In Space?* New York: Tom Doherty Books, 1985.

INDEX

SAYVILLF LIBRARY
11 COLLINS AVE
SAYVILLE, NY 11782

AUG 26 1998